The 101 Best iMac2020 Tips, Stunts and Timesavers

Apple iMac2020 Guide for Busy People

Grace Wealth

Contents

Gallery View
Scrubber bar

INTRODUCTION

With the introduction of MacOS Catalina, users now have the opportunity to explore the full potential of Mac. Interestingly, Mac performs several functions than you know. Mac and MacBook PCs make use of their local software, which are more efficient than Windows 10 and their costly third-party tools.

One of the significant advantages of using a Mac is that you don't have to set up a ton of third-party apps that are typical of Windows devices — everything just works. Using Mac's native software, you can carry out some light photoshop work, integrate various PDFs, or even sign on some files. So, we have put up with a list of 100 valuable Mac tips and advice to help you find out what your Mac can do.

This quickly comprehensible list contains the top 100 Mac ideas, which are arranged into slides of bite-size.

1.   Speak to your Mac, and listen

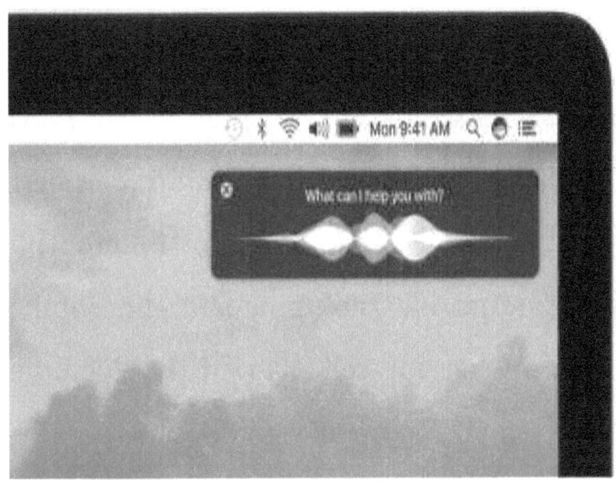

Before macOS Sierra decided to launch in 2016,

Mac's ability to listen to you and respond through

Dictation had been remarkable. That was overtaken
by the arrival of Siri on Apple's Mac lineup.

You should either press and hold Command and
Space for a few moments, or just press the Siri key

on your Dock or Menu Bar and call the same Siri
you've become used to on your iPhone.

If you've got a new Mac (like the IMac)

you should simply say _Hi Siri.' The upgraded Siri is a valuable bonus.

In addition to the queries you generally ask, such as the climatic conditions or who play in the playoff game, Siri on macOS Mojave and Catalina can switch system functionality such as Wi-Fi or Bluetooth, or pull up individual files contained in the database depending on what you tell it about the document. Siri will also get you to open applications.

Simply tap _Command+Space,' and ask.

2. Unit Conversions in Spotlight

Simple Spotlight calculations are popular already, but with macOS High Sierra, you can do even better: Unit conversions. When needed, you can do specific unit conversions — say —13 stone in pounds‖—but you can also just type in the quantity and unit you want to convert, and your Mac will recommend not only the likely conversion but also a few options.

Type something like _$1,299,' and you will be given the value in the native language you selected under System Preferences Language and

Region panel (i.e., Pounds Sterling). Afterward, the screen will display further results, showing Yen, Euros, and so on. You can also type the particular currency you're seeking for, such as —$1,299 to AUD‖ if the exchange rate you're looking for doesn't show up.

3. Take Screenshots of any size

Screen captures can be a hassle for Windows users. You can either use the PrtSc button to grab your screen as a whole or use the Snipping Tools to catch just one piece. Individual keypads aren't consistent with the shortcut, of course, and launching a dedicated app to take a screenshot is a bit of trouble. Fortunately, the operation on a Mac is automated.

Taking a pic of your display surface is easy, just press Shift + Command + 3 simultaneously, and the screengrab will be stored on your home screen. The alternative is Shift + Command + 4 with the same output tab if you only want a section of the display.

When using Shift + Command + 4 to choose a region of the screen, if you touch the spacebar, the icon transforms into a camera.

You can tap on any open window after this to get a snapshot of just that window or layout feature, such as the dock or navigation menu. Shift + Command + 5, an underrated option, creates an interface that allows you to record a part of your display or screen.

4. Run Windows

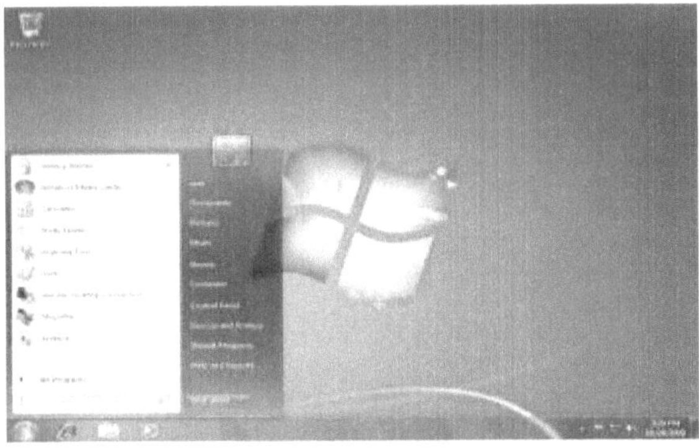

No self-respecting Mac follower needs to operate Windows. But often it's useful, whether you're playing the new games or running a small piece application similar to Mac.

You can either operate windows across macOS with virtualization software like Parallels Desktop, VMware Fusion, or VirtualBox or use Boot Camp Assistant (in your Utility folder) to separate your hard drive to run windows on and run it full throttle on your computer.

Finally, if you've got a flashy new MacBookPro with the Touch Bar, press _shift-Command-6' to take a snapshot of that small OLED strip. Whatever the case, taking a screenshot on a Mac, involves just remembering a few different keyboard shortcuts.

Furthermore, with macOS Mojave and Catalina, a sample of the screenshot displays at the lower right corner of the screen each moment you take a screenshot. To get a markup window, add information to the picture, and save them, you can click on this teaser. It's particularly nifty productivity feature.

5. Type exotic characters

6. Automatically hide and show the menu bar

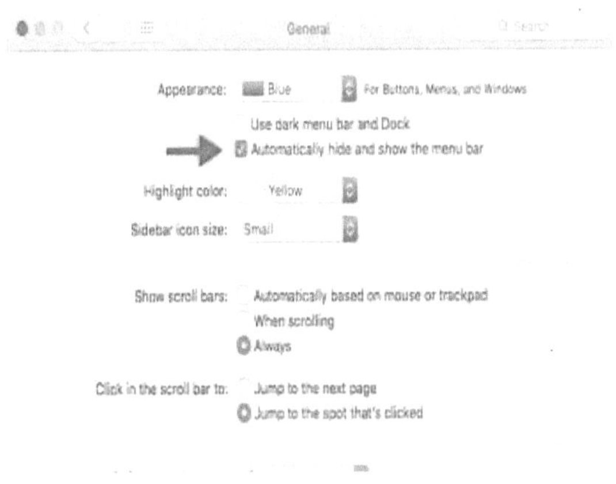

Since Mac was launched in 1984, the menu bar has been a constant feature. But ever since OS X EI Capitan, you can conceal the menu bar. Open system preferences, choose General, and then click 'Automatically hide and show the menu bar.'

When you click on the box, the menu bar will appear, and you can guide your mouse towards the top so you can get all the menus.

You would be surprised at the fascinating array of interesting characters you can type on your Mac in addition to all the letters and symbols that you see on your keyboard. For words with accents like café which you are already familiar with, Mac offers much more.

Simply go to the Edit option on your menu of the most app, and you'll see Special Characters at the bottom. This panel will then give you access to a wide range of symbols that you can drag into your documents- not all apps or operating systems support them. But these are mostly parts of the

Cross-platform Unicode Standard. You may see more so you can click on the cog to reveal more.

Emojis (fun, colorful characters that are only available in OS X 10.7) is a notable exception to the cross-platform world. They are not alone in Apple, but except your recipient may not be able to see them.

7. Rename files in Batches

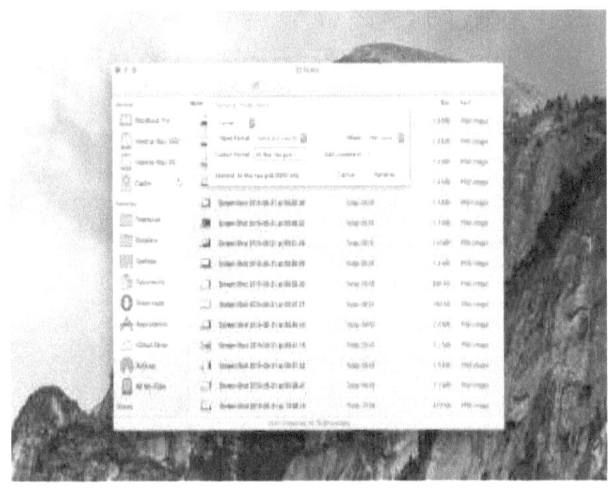

In OS X releases before Yosemite, renaming an occasion of reports quickly either concluded outcast programming or moving your rename content using something like Automatic or AppleScript. These days, regardless, you can necessarily pick a get-together of records and then select Rename either from the right-click sensible menu or beginning from the drop button set apart with a machine gear-piece picture in Finder windows. Right when you do, you get to decide to include content, override content, or apply an approach, for instance, a name and an along these lines developing counter.

8. Sign into a PDF Doc

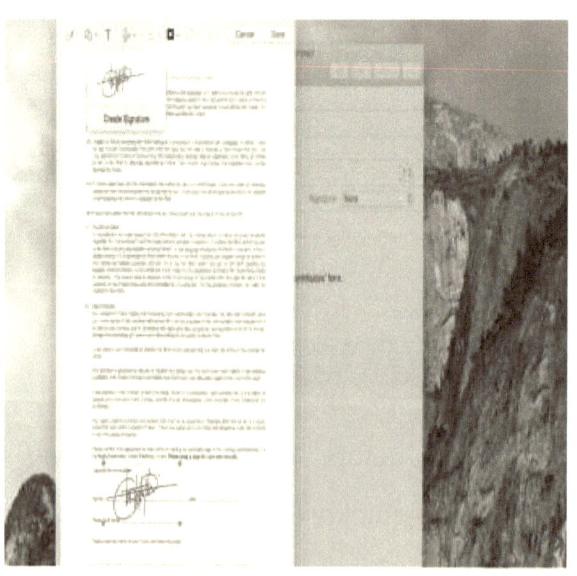

10

It might be the 21st century, yet we're using squiggles on a touch of paper to agree to all methods of things. If you are aware of a PDF to sign, in any case, you don't have to fuss about printing it, stamping it, by then separating it legitimately in Mail.

Drag a PDF into the email you're sending, float over it, then at the upper right, you'll see a little catch appear. Snap it, and you get an extent of Markup options, including one for stamping records. Besides, you can either incorporate your imprint by holding a stamped bit of paper up to the webcam on your Mac - and it makes a magnificent appearance of expelling it of the establishment - or by drawing on your trackpad.

Have you got an iPad pointer? Try using that as opposed to your finger.

9. Easy Sharing With Friends

In different places in OS X and MacOS, you will see the option of sharing things to friends and contacts from a little Share button that seems like an arrow moving out of a box. The best piece is that Macs screen take records of how and whom you consistently share stuff with.

In case you love to share funny kinds of stuff or link with a friend and eavesdropping records to a partner sitting near you, these choices will be at the base of the share menu so that it is easier to choose the option next time you need to.

10. Image Capture

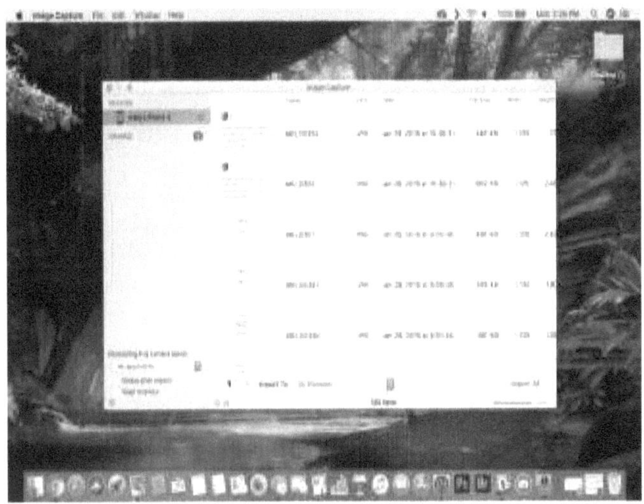

Even though you could import photographs from your iPhone or DSLR physically utilizing a couple of Finder windows, a more straightforward method to do so is by utilizing Image Capture. The longstanding feature is not strange to macOS, yet a staggering number of Mac newcomers has neglected it. In it, you can decide to import the entirety of your camera's photographs without a moment's delay, straightforwardly to the organizer based on your personal preference, or even better; you can single out which pictures to store on your Mac while concluding whether to keep or erase the firsts individually.

Also, you can likewise interface remotely to a scanner to import examined records or photographs of your choice. You can likewise connect your camera to any macOS application that you need. So on the off chance that you need Photoshop to open each time you associate your iPhone, Image Capture can be designed to get that going

11. Split Screen Use

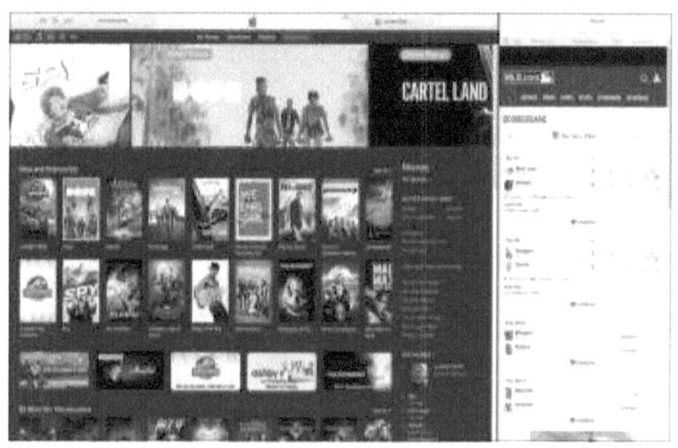

Working with two windows or applications, one close to the next, just ended up being much more

straightforward since OS X 10.11 El Capitan, because of Split Screen. In case you're still on macOS Mojave, you can hold down a left-click on an application's green enlarged button in the upper left-hand side, by then drag it to be arranged on the left or right-hand side of the introduction.

If you have MacOS Catalina presented, it's, to some degree, uncommon. You simply left-snap and hold tight that green most outrageous catch, which draws out a dropdown menu in which you can choose to Enter Full Screen, Tile Window to Left of Screen, or Tile Window to Right of screen. Moreover, if you have a helper screen, this menu will similarly give you the decision to move the dynamic window to that screen.

Any way you do it, you'll by then need to pick a second open window or application to snap to the opposite side. Split Screen mists the launcher and OS X's Menu Bar, so you get more screenland and fewer interferences.

Dividing the separating lines between the two applications lets you make them more diminutive or more significant, anyway not by much.

In any case, this can end up helping keep an eye out for live information, for instance, sports scores toward one side while being beneficial on the other.

12. Annotate PDFs and images

The preview is an incredibly fascinating tool. It can only get more potent on MacOS Mojave. Apart from letting you preview PDF's and pictures, preview allow for different annotation for PDF that is user friendly with Adobe's PDF app and Acrobat that are used by windows users and companies, so that it is easier to share annotated document among colleagues, not minding the platform they choose to use.

Just ensure that the Edit toolbar is not hidden (from the menu), and you'll see the variety of options for creating shapes and drawing things with bubbles

and other tools. And there are various other options
to highlight and text in different colors,
strikethrough, etc.

13. Choose Your folder and file icons

As a Mac customer, you should be used to everything
being bright and beautiful. Taking everything into
account, the graphical UI has been a selling point for
Apple PCs since the advent of Macintosh. So you
don't bother with your experience interrupted by

icons that you don't like when it can be easily changed to your preferred images.

In reality, doing this is less difficult than you might assume. And you don't need to download a thirdparty program that is sketched just to transform the thumbnail images that show up when you save important things to the desktop of your PC. What you should do is to click on the document and select 'Get Info' and then copy the preview image that you need preview (or your editing image app). The next step is to click the current thumbnail in the 'Get Info' window and press Command + V to paste the image from your editor to the file of the info window. Guess what? Your files are now looking exactly the way you want it to look- beautiful and viably prominent!

14. Crop and Tweak Images

One of the most underestimated applications on macOS is the preview. The preview is tremendously astonishing and a great fascination. It can perform tasks that we'd normally be stuck when using a sophisticated like Photoshop for.

Believe me, when you open an image in preview and check out the application's menus and interface, you'll be amazed to see exactly what it's set up to do. For example, you can alter your image- crop your image. After you choose your image, you can draw a rectangular section that you want to crop. You can either hit Command+K or choose Crop from the

Tools menu to do this. Another way to do this, is to show the Edit Toolbar and decide to take on a selection that is more complex either with the Instant Alpha gadget or use the Smart Lasso.

15. Create a Keyboard Shortcut

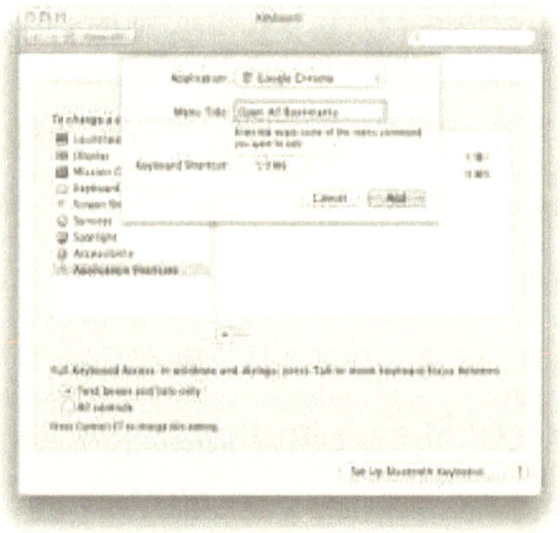

You can save a lot of time using shortcuts, yet, you are not limited to the shortcut that comes along with your system; if there's a particular menu you use continually that doesn't have a shortcut, you can create one by yourself.

Go to System Preferences > Keyboard > App Shortcuts. Click the button to input a new shortcut. You can pick which application you want to apply it to (beginning from the drop list). You should know the particular name of the menu request to type into the accompanying box, including the correct case and any one of a kind characters, even ellipses. Finally, pick an uncommon key mix to bring the request, and then click.

16. Find your Forgotten Wi-Fi Password

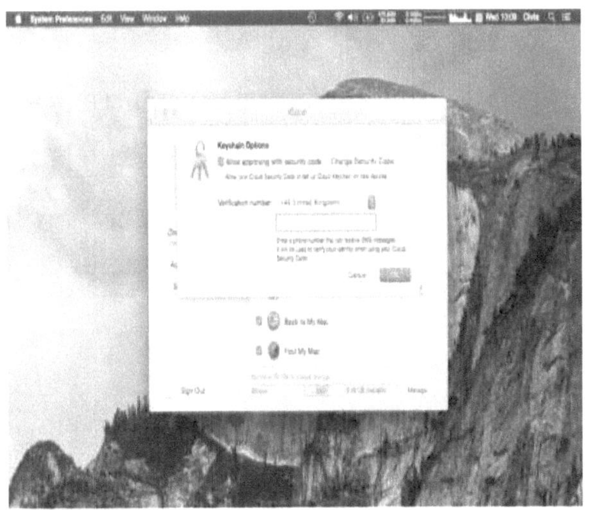

The outstanding difference in Macs that separate it from other PCs is its ability to remember every one of your passwords and magically give it back to you if you are using an Apple feature called Keychain. Keychain Access (unique programming) is the in-built software that comes with Keychain. This is where a lot of your private accounts and details are stored. You'd be fascinated, but then, this area can only be easily accessed with WiFi connections.

If you ever end up in another spot, or if somehow, you can't remember your WiFi password, you can use Keychain Access on your Mac to find it. The procedure is uncomplicated and easy: just open up Keychain Access by looking for it in Spotlight, look for the name of the connection and click on the iCloud Keychain that aligns with the SSID you're looking for.

Starting there, click 'Show password' and enter the Keychain password that you set previously. You'll by then be invited by the WiFi password that you're too anxious to ask for. For future reference, in any case, you are better off asking for help from others.

17. Use Automator For Speed

Automator is a mechanical assembly fused with OS X that enables you to produce your work procedures of requests, making complex endeavors significantly easier later on. Use it to develop your little apps that carry out a specific task, to make a work procedure to change several bunches of files, or to make new services, which are functions that you can access just by clicking on it. You could use Automator to rename endless files, to transfer images to another file type, to turn content files into audio files, and a lot more.

• To make something in Automator, open it, then pick what sort of thing you have to make: each is useful in different conditions, so click on them to see description. Select the one you need and Choose (or open an old Automator file).

• Start making the methods for your work procedure by pulling Actions from the left-hand side of the screen to the unfilled space on the right-hand side. Actions are grouped by application and file type, or you can search for something at the top. Just snap an Action's name to see what it does.

• Once you've built up your work procedure, you can click Run in the upper right corner to test it (anyway, you won't have the alternative to test everything this way totally). If there are any issues, the part where it bombarded will have a red cross near it, and the log underneath will explain any alarms.

18. See Another Person's PC

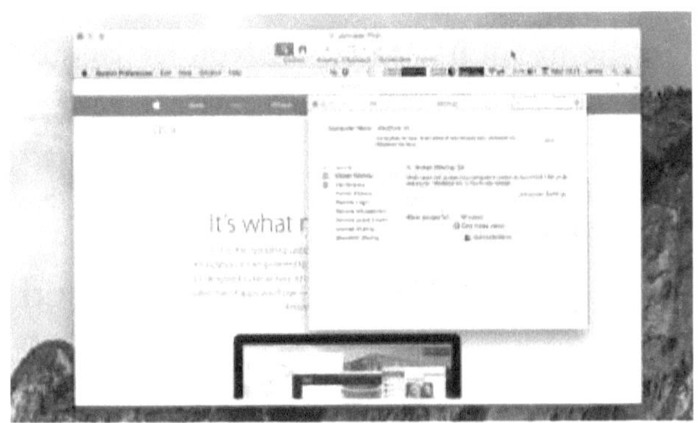

One amazingly basic way to deal with viewing someone else's screen or even control their Mac is over the web (this is precious if you're endeavoring to troubleshoot their PC issues). Launch Screen Sharing utilizing searching for it with Spotlight and then entering the Apple ID of the individual you're endeavoring to contact. If you or they don't have any colleague with it, just have them look in the iCloud pane of System Preferences. Moreover, while you're on that screen, be sure they have screen Sharing engaged in the Sharing pane of System Preferences.

They'll be asked to permit you to see their screen, and they too can then tap on the screen sharing image in the menu bar and grant you the ability to in every way that matters, remotely control their mouse and reassure also.

19. Change How Notifications are grouped

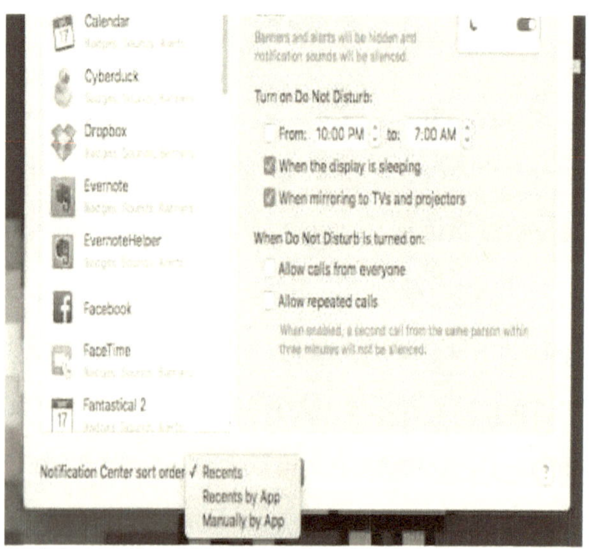

Years before, before El Capitan, OS X defaulted to categorizing items in Notification Center by the application. But now Apple has changed it up and now groups them by date. For example, all of your notification from today will show up together, which can be useful for seeing what you missed while you were away.

If you lean toward the old per-application gathering, nonetheless, go to System Preferences > Notifications, by then change it to the sort order of your preference: search for the pop-up menu named "Notification Center sort order." Browse around the different other options and see which one works for you.

20. Create Message threads

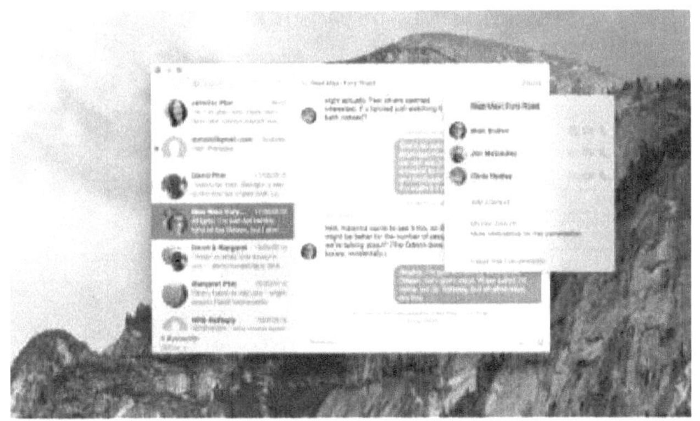

In case you have tons of iMessage conversations going on at some irregular times, it might be quite easy not to remember who said what, where, and when, which is especially obvious in case you ordinarily use multi-people talks and mix work and fun. Since the invention of OS X Yosemite, it has become simpler; you can name group chats by clicking Details at the upper right, by then forming a name at the top.

You could do this for particular, nonessential conversations ("Meeting up for the Cup Final this week's end" or "Advancement activity for the new dispatch"). Or then again, you can use iMessage like and old IRC chatroom, making one called "Talk," which you and your dear sidekicks can reliably fly in for some expansive visit.

21. **Record your iPhone or iPad's screen**

With Yosemite, you can record whatever happens on the screen of the device. Creators need to display the applications and games they build and it's great for things like creating minimal instructional activities or even essentially recording a bug so you can bolster a specialist or an association fix it.

To use this component, you partner your iOS device up to your Mac using its connection, by then dispatch QuickTime Player. Then pick New Movie Recording from the File menu and a while later if it's not successfully picked for you, pick your related iOS contraption as the 'camera' source beginning from the drop menu near the record button.

Pick whether you have to record sound (either from a certain or external mic or the sound the iOS device itself is making) from a comparable menu, by then snap the recorded image. At the point when you're set, you can trim the catch (T) and a short time later viably share it too, for example, YouTube.

22. Adjust the volume a little

Right, when you experience the volume and down keys on your Mac's comfort, the difference between one tap and the accompanying can truly be genuinely enormous – especially if you're driving some significant outside speakers. Hold down ⌥ and ⇧ as you tap those keys, be that as it may, and the enlargements become much more diminutive.

Here's a prize tip: if the perceptible analysis when you change the volume makes you crazy, you can turn it off in System Preferences, anyway here's the sharp piece – you can by chance flip it back on by holding when you adjust the volume – advantageous when you're dubious about whether your Mac isn't making.

23. Share SMSs on your MAC

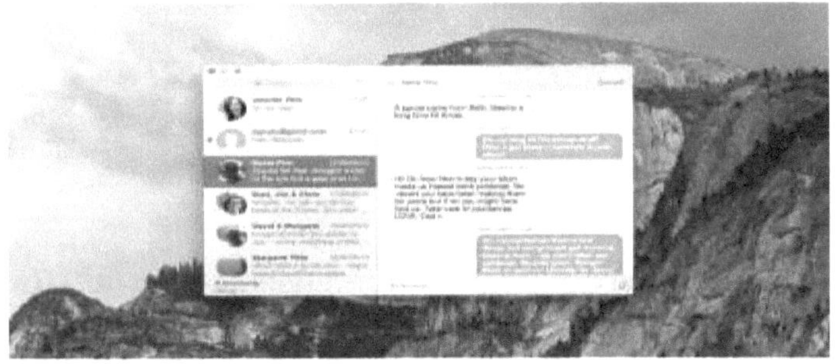

Right when someone sends an SMS – a text in the primary mobile phone sense – to your iPhone, it appears in a green air pocket instead of a blue one, as it would be if someone sends you an iMessage. At the time before the creation Yosemite, SMSs would simply appear on your iPhone, where you'd have to peck out an answer, but at this point, you can have them come into your Mac or various iOS devices when they appear so you can reply to them from there.

24. Choose Your Type Of Screenshot

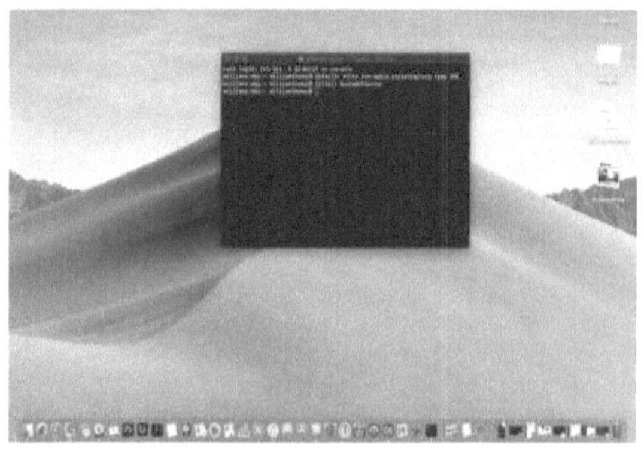

If you always love taking screenshots – at whatever point you see something critical, astute, or charming that you need to save something for your records or send to your friends. Even though on macOS

Mojave, your screenshots are defaulted to save as PNGs, you can change that.

In case you have to save your Screenshots as JPGs, head into Terminal and type 'defaults make com.apple. Screen capture types JPG' by then Enter. At the point when that is done, the change will become compelling once you restart your Mac. In case you can barely wait that long, you can

force the change by typing "KillAllSystemUIServer" and hit enter, and the UI will restart.

25. Share your purchases with your relatives

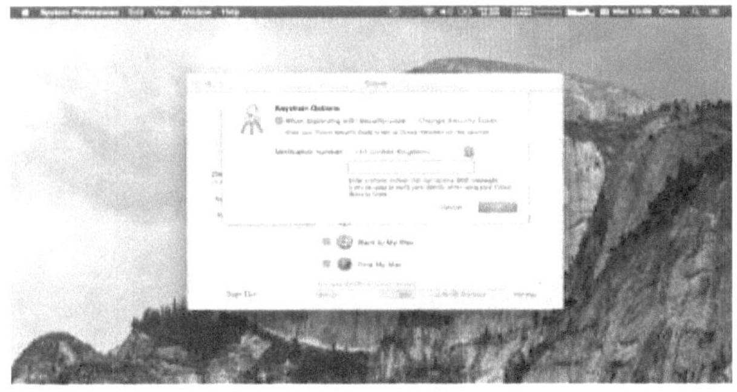

Up to six people in a comparable family can share purchases through the macOS Family Sharing component. As a parent, this is tough because it permits you to underwrite or excuse App Store purchases by kids – and you'll get various focal points, for instance, viably having the choice to see where everyone is, and getting a typical family plan.

It's not hard to set up, too. Go to the iCloud territory of System Preferences and click Set Up Family, by then follow the prompts.

It's a lot easier in case you have climbed to macOS Catalina. You ought to just go to System Preferences, and snap-on Family Sharing arranged near Apple ID.

26. Switch audio source/output from the menu bar

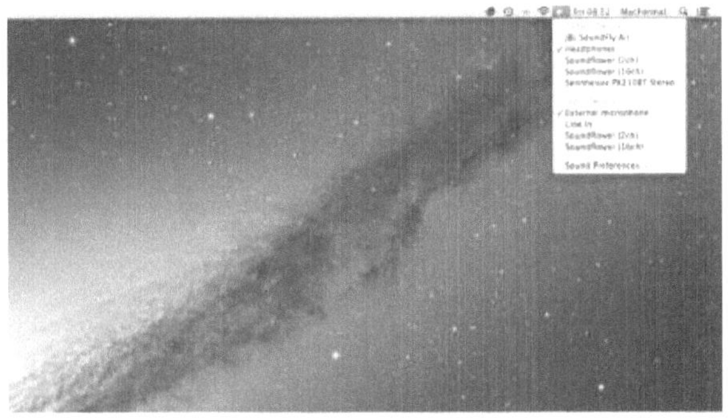

In case you have speakers or headphones set up with your Mac. If you have a headset or beneficiary related, you may end up expecting to switch between different information sources or yields, anyway, this doesn't have to mean a walk to System Preferences each time.

Just hold Option and snap the volume specialist in the menu bar (or push on one of the volumes secured on your reassure).

This will raise an overview of sound data sources and yields. You would then have the option to pick the one you need. Recollect be that as it may, that it's limited in the proportion of yields it can appear, so this decision is compelling for continuously complex courses of action.

27. Use your iPad as a secondary Mac display

Have you felt like your PC's introduction just doesn't offer enough show any more extended for the rest of the job that needs to be done? Apple understands, which is the explanation the association uncovered its Sidecar remember for its latest macOS, macOS Catalina. This allows iPad's that just been relaxing around on your footrest more prominent helpfulness in your regular.

Before you start, guarantee that you have macOS Catalina presented on your Mac and the latest iPadOS presented on your iPad. Moreover, you ought to be set apart into iCloud on the two contraptions using a comparative Apple ID. All in all, guarantee that you have both Bluetooth and WiFi turned on.

To use Sidecar, essentially follow these methods: First, click the Airplay image in the menu bar on your PC by then select the iPad you'd like to use. This lets you partner with the two devices remotely. To use a wired affiliation, just interface the two with a decent connection.

At the point when the two are related, whether or not remotely or through connection, the Sidecar image will override the Airplay image on the menu bar. Snap the Sidecar image, and select "Use As Separate Display" in case you have to utilize it as a comprehensive grandstand or "Mirror Built-in Retina Display" to use it as a reflected introduction. Also, there you go! You would now have the option to use your iPad as an assistant introduction. Review, to abuse this segment, you ought to have a Mac PC released in 2016 or later and an Apple pencil immaculate iPad model.

28. Cure an insomniac Mac

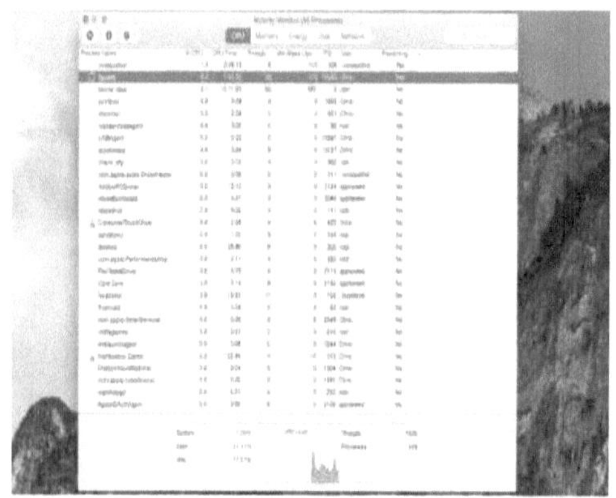

You may observe that now and again when you close your MacBook's spread or pick Sleep from the Apple menu on your iMac or Mac littler than common that it valiantly won't rest.

Luckily, it's not hard to get to the base of this issue with your Mac. Since the time OS X Yosemite, you can investigate the View > Column menu when you're on Activity Monitor's CPU tab to show a section of methodology that is thwarting rest. Snap this segment header to sort by it, and a while later you can without a very remarkable stretch find which applications are keeping your Mac attentive, by then quit them if necessary.

29. Store anything you like in iCloud Drive

It used to be the circumstance that the principle records you could store on iCloud were from exceptionally collected applications, for instance, Apple's iWork suite, however, at this point, we have the updated iCloud Drive in macOS Sierra.

By and by, in macOS High Sierra, you can toss any record you like onto either the Desktop or

Documents envelope, despite the iCloud Drive image in the Finder sidebar, and those records and coordinators will be coordinated up normally. Those of a kind, "supported" applications notwithstanding everything get their envelopes, any way you can make your own or put things into the iCloudDrive free by methods for the Desktop and Documents coordinators.

All of those records will conform to various Macs set apart in with your Apple ID (to the extent that you've engaged iCloud Drive on them) and will, in like manner, be available through icloud.com. On iOS, applications that can use iCloud will regularly default to opening reports from their extraordinary envelope, anyway should in like manner license you to scrutinize through your entire iCloud Drive to open records set aside elsewhere.

30. Quick searching within sites

There's a cool, gravely grasped component in Safari since Yosemite: the limit quickly to peer inside express goals straightforwardly from Safari's request bar. How it's capacities are at present: assume you go to amazon.com and examine for 'MacBook.' What truly happens is that you're redirected to another URL that looks something like this:

http://www.amazon.com/s/ref=nb_sb_noss_2?url

=search-alias%3Daps   HYPERLINK

"http://www.amazon.com/s/ref=nb_sb_noss_2?ur l=search-alias%3Daps&field-

keywords=macbook"& HYPERLINK

"http://www.amazon.com/s/ref=nb_sb_noss_2?ur
l=search-
alias%3Daps&fieldkeywords=macbook"field-
keywords=macbook.

http://www.amazon.com/s/ref=nb_sb_noss_2?url

=search-alias%3Daps   HYPERLINK

"http://www.amazon.com/s/ref=nb_sb_noss_2?ur
l=search-alias%3Daps&field-keywords=imac"&

HYPERLINK

"http://www.amazon.com/s/ref=nb_sb_noss_2?ur
l=search-alias%3Daps&field-
keywords=imac"fieldkeywords=imac.

To get that moving, you ought to just sort 'amazon iMac' into Safari's request bar, and after that, you'll see one of the decisions is 'Mission amazon.com for iMac'; click on this, and you'll go straightforward to the results.

You have to do an interest – any request – in a site first before Safari can see the language structure for a chase string, anyway when you do, you'll see the goals recorded in the Search tab of Safari's tendencies.

You can even sort just a bit of the goal site's URL.

To the extent that you've looked once on

Wikipedia, for example, you can type 'wiki apple,' and you'll see the choice to examine Wikipedia for

"apple."

31. Share (some) contact details

You can, without a very remarkable stretch, send someone your contact nuances either by doing it as it was done in past times worth remembering of pulling a contact card out of the Contacts application and subsequently affixing it to an email, say or by using the new Share orders since Yosemite. Yet, the issue with this central strategy is that you may have information on your card you needn't bother with others to have.

For example, you may have described a relationship with your life accomplice so that on your iPhone, you can say "establish a connection with my significant other" without showing who you mean. You should keep that information covered up for security reasons.

By and by, it's straightforward. In Contacts' tendencies, click vCard then Enable private me card. By and by, when you go to your Me card in Contacts – and you may need to portray one first – and click Edit, you get a movement of checkboxes near each field to show whether it would be consolidated when you share a card.

32. Close tabs left open on other devices

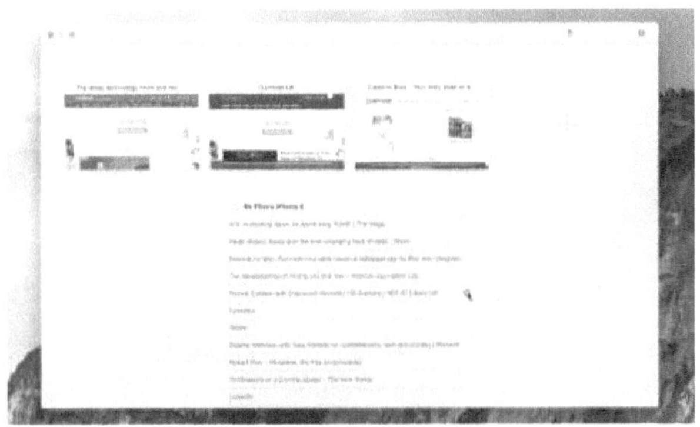

Whether or not you just unexpectedly recognized that you've left a dodgy tab open on an iPad you've as of late given to a partner or considering the way that it's just totally less difficult to experience and close a ton of tabs on your Mac rather than on an iOS device, you ought to understand that you can close tabs open on any device set apart into your Apple ID from Safari since Yosemite.

Snap the image that seems like two covering squares in Safari (or pick Show All Tabs from the View menu), and you'll see all your open tabs on the sum of your devices. Buy over each, and you'll see a close-by get you can click. (This also works from iOS to Mac; swipe alternative to left on a cloud tab in its tab view and tap Delete; that tab will by then be closed on the Mac.)

33. Get connected to the web via your iPhone

iPhones are designed with a feature that empowers you to share their 3G/4G "mobile broadband connection" with other gadgets(your network's operator must permit this). This feature makes going online from your Mac easy and accessible from wherever and whenever. There are 3 ways by which you can connect your Mac and iPhone to share signal: Wi-Fi, USB & Bluetooth.

Firstly, navigate to the "Personal Hotspot option" in your iPhone's Settings, and switch it on. If you want Wi-Fi connection, you have to locate the WiFi network made by your iPhone in the "Mac Wi-Fi options"; you should select it then type-in the secret word displayed on the iPhone.

For the USB connection, plug together your iPhone and your Mac. You ought to get a prompt that directs you to the "Network section" in "System Preferences." From there, you can choose the iPhone. For your Bluetooth connection, initiate Bluetooth on the two gadgets and pair them together. After that, the connection option will be displayed again in "System Preferences >

Network."

34. Utilize "Home Sharing" when you want to share your "iTunes library."

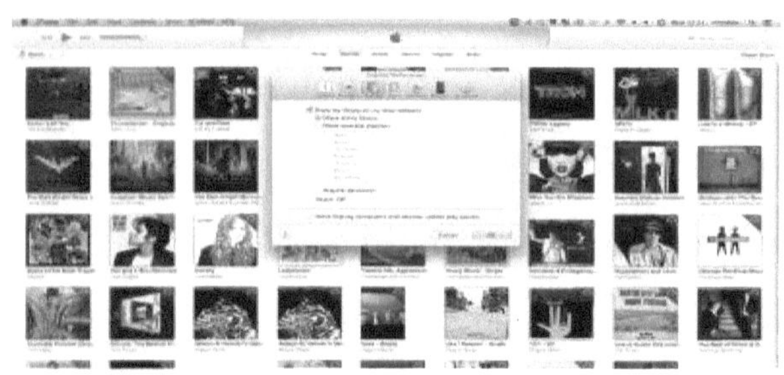

It's a common occurrence for individuals in a family or a shared apartment to share movies, music, and TV shows with one another. You can do this effectively using Home Sharing. Simply navigate to System Preferences, then select Sharing and tick the box tagged "Home Sharing."

To share your media files with your friends and relatives who are not registered with Apple ID, mark "share media with guests." To keep your device secured, you can restrain access to your device's library by tapping Options; after that, proceed to create a password. If that is not done, then everybody will have access to your library.

35. Print to any accessible printer

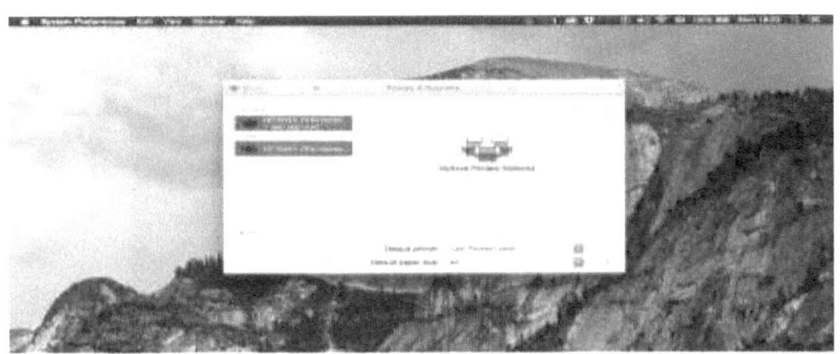

Sometimes it gets very irritating when you have to wait for another person to print out enormous files when you're running short on time. This here is a tip to remedy such situations if there are multiple printers available. From System Preferences, go to "Print and Fax" (or Printers and Scanners for the latest models of OS X). There you can choose numerous printers and build a "Printer Pool."

You would then be able to choose this Pool from the "print dialogue" in applications rather than your printers. Also, if one printer is being used, the Mac will naturally send the file to any free printer in the Pool – no pausing!

36. Get wireless video & audio using AirPlay

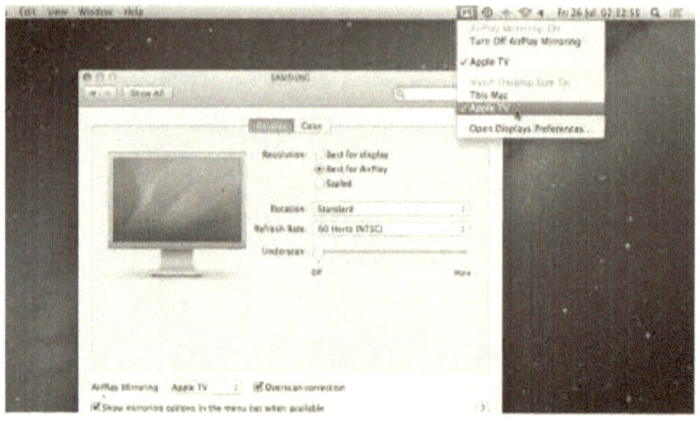

AirPlay is a feature from Apple that allows you to stream video and audio inside your home, and it's accessible on both Macs and iOS gadgets. Most Macs can stream audio files to your AirPlay speakers; however, the updated Macs can likewise reflect the displays to your Apple TV. With that, you'll be able to display visuals on the widescreen.

To access simple AirPlay services from "Apple Music & TV," all you have to do is to tap its image (the rectangle that has a triangle cutting inside it) then pick where you desire to send the audio file. If you need the entirety of your device's audio to originate from your speakers rather than just music, hold

Option then tap a "volume control key" to unlock "Sound Preferences." From there, you can pick an output or utilize the "Menu bar tip" we previously referenced.

In the case whereby an Apple TV shares the same network with your Mac, you'll, by default, see an AirPlay symbol within the menu bar. To begin screen mirroring, pick it and tap on your Apple TV's name.

37. Sharing a printer with different Macs

The network printers have become very helpful as they allow anybody on the network to print wirelessly. In a situation whereby you have an incredible printer previously linked with your Mac and would prefer not to supplant it, you could still enjoy a similar comfort. From System Preferences, go to Sharing then tick on the "Printer Sharing service."

Once you're here, you'll get a screen from which you can choose the printer to share, as well as determine who can utilize it. Once the settings are completed, every Mac on your network can print to that printer from the "print dialogue." However, the Mac to which your printer is connected has to be switched on.

38. Create a "Guest User account" in your Mac

As you presumably know, your Apple device allows the addition of numerous users to the Mac. That enables each individual in your office, shop or home, to get their own working space and arrange things just the way they want. However, you can create another type of account: The Guest account.

Switch this function on in "System Preferences"> "Users and Groups," from there you'll be given the Guest alternative in the login section. Anybody can utilize it (passwords aren't required); however, once they're done, all that they did will be cleaned-out.

This is useful to not only the Mac-users in spare rooms or foyers, but also to the other companions or associate who could say, "Could you maybe lend me your Mac for a moment to carry out some tasks?"

For security reasons, you likely should switch-off "Automatic login" and configure your "Security and Privacy settings" to request for a password after every four seconds of screensaver/sleep time. With such measures, you can be certain no one will have the opportunity to get to your stuff; however, when they attempt to utilize your Mac, they'll be offered the choice of exchanging client and would then be able to pick Guest.

39. With Safari, you can hide your tracks

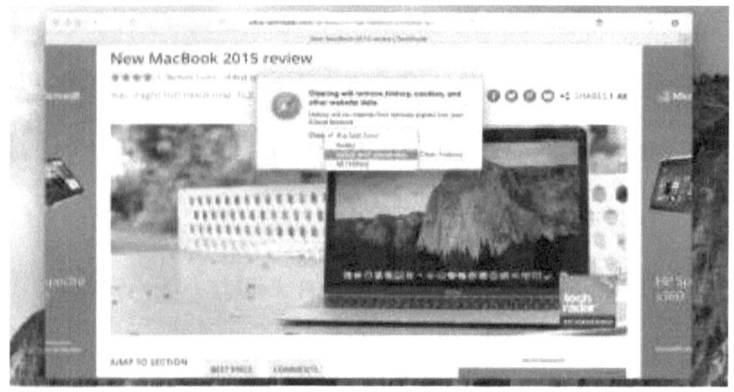

Initially, with the Safari, if you needed to erase history & caches, the only option available was the

"nuclear option," which would wipe-out everything. However, enter Yosemite, now you can pick "Clear History" & "Website Data" from your computer's Safari History menu. From there, you can choose to cover your tracks using the options (clear data from the past hour, today, and "today & yesterday). You can also, as in the past, clear from all time. The new Option clears your browsing history from all gadgets registered into the iCloud account.

40. Restrain what somebody can do as well as when

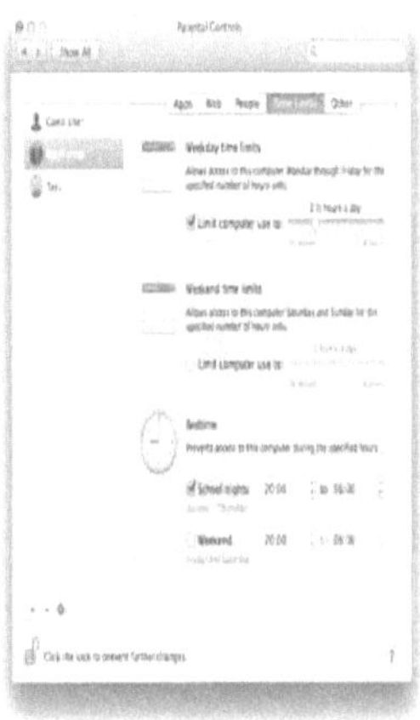

The "Parental Controls" in OS X are basic, yet there is a lot of alternatives in it – most of them are valuable for different things apart from forestalling underage access. You can restrain the usage of your PC use to a specific timeframe each day. You could set a 'sleep time' which will be the time when nobody can utilize your computer. Also, you can restrain the "Finder functions" and the apps that a user can work with at a time, and more. For instance, you can deny a particular user from adjusting the Dock or resetting a new password.

41. Email enormous files

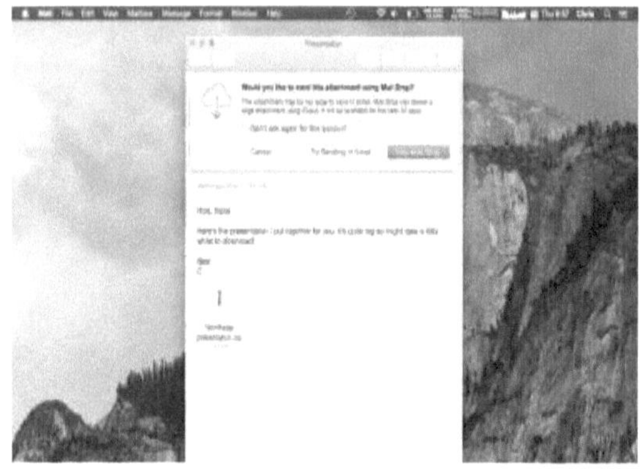

The Email isn't generally designed for the transferring of files; however, the truth is everyone does it. The thing is that most email suppliers generally won't allow you to send attachments that are bigger than a specific size (regularly just a couple of megabytes), so it's usually a bad idea trying to send enormous documents over Email.

However, since Yosemite (with Mail and with the webmail variant of Mail from "icloud.com, "you can now send big-sized email documents (about 5GB).

The actual event is that your Mail gets transferred to iCloud, and afterward, the recipient receives a link. Note that the recipient has 30 days to download the file.

If the receiver is utilizing Mail on "Yosemite/icloud.com," they'll simply get the documentwithin their Email as opposed to getting a link.

42. Toss documents from your Mac into your iPhone

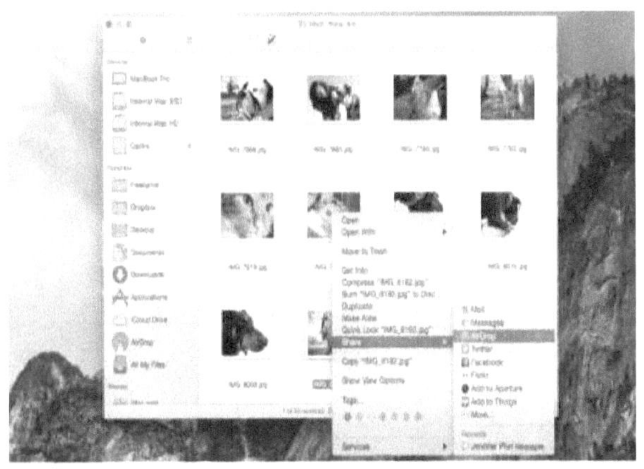

Remember that, with an advanced Mac built with "Bluetooth 4.0" and an updated iOS gadget like the iPhone 5 model or a recent one, you can conveniently send documents in your Mac into your iOS gadget utilizing AirDrop.

The fastest method to perform this is to right-tap on the document you are sending and select AirDrop (from the Messages fly-out menu) then select the gadget you need to send it to.

You can switch On AirDrop from the "Control Center" of your iOS gadget.

43. Quickly locate the menu bar utilizing Help

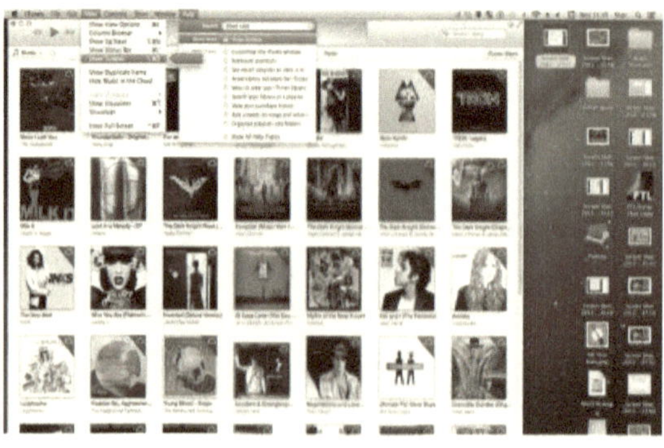

Some applications contain more "menu Bar options" than you can want to monitor, however as opposed to looking through every drop-down physically, you can utilize the last "Help menu" to quicken the process. It comprises of a search box through which you can enter the initials of the Option you're searching for.

Results are displayed below it, and drifting over results will display the menu it's in, or users can simply tap the result to choose it.

44. Change the size of your windows just like an expert at window-resizing

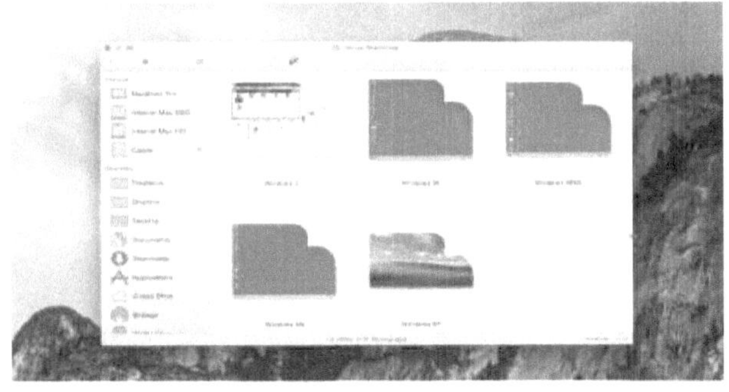

Since Yosemite, tapping the green Tab at the upper left of your window, presently takes your windows full screen instead of expanding it, however, you can now restore the old conduct by pressing down on ⌥ as you float across the green Tab. There's more you can do, though. Hold on ⌥ while you resize a side of the window as the other side of the window resizes as well. Hold ⇧ to enable the window to resize relatively, adjusted to the edge on the opposite side (this may sound somewhat confounding, but when you attempt, it makes sense).

You can also press down on ⌥ and ⇧ while changing the size of a window so that the entire thing recoils down relatively around the middle. Set up everything so you can tap the green Tab to create a window and fill your screen to resize a particular edge.

45. Past content without maintaining the format

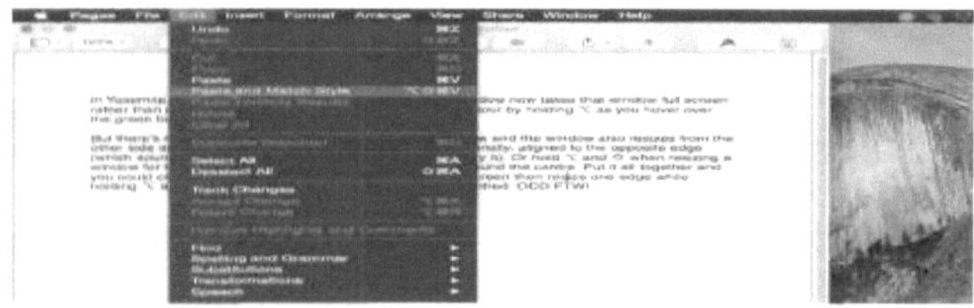

When copying content from certain applications, and particularly from the internet, you will typically duplicate its formatting, for example, the content size, font style, etc. Once you paste this in a content field like an email, it appears improperly, and that can make things difficult to read.

To paste content without its initial formatting (to allow for proper readability of what you're pasting into), rather than tapping Command+V, tap Option+Shift+Command+V.

The "Microsoft Word" has a "paste Special "or

"paste & Match Style" menu for the same purpose.

46. Prepare things instantly at sign in

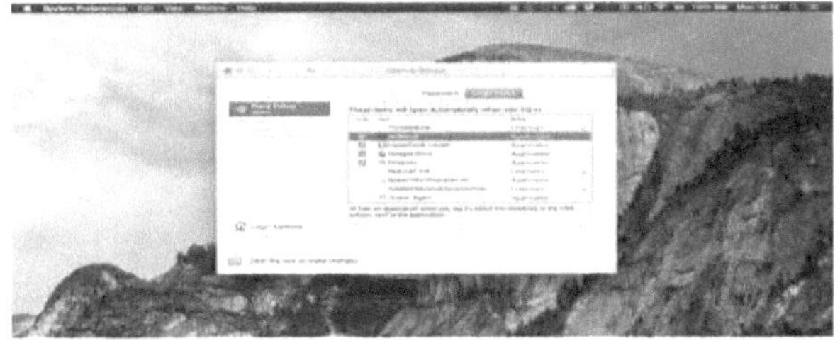

There are some applications that users generally need to open whenever they fire up the Mac, and one can configure this in "System Preferences." Navigate to Users and ensure your account is featured, then tap "Login Items."

From there, tap "the +," and you can pick your favorite apps or simply whatever else you want to be opened when you fire-up your Mac. Once the apps have been added, you can utilize the checkboxes option to conceal it if you want, however, in the background, it'll run.

Be cautious while doing this because if you have a lot of apps running immediately, you fire up your Mac can make it slow. Thus, if you have to speed things up, press Shift so that OS X/macOS will log you in and suppress the apps.

47. Control your windows

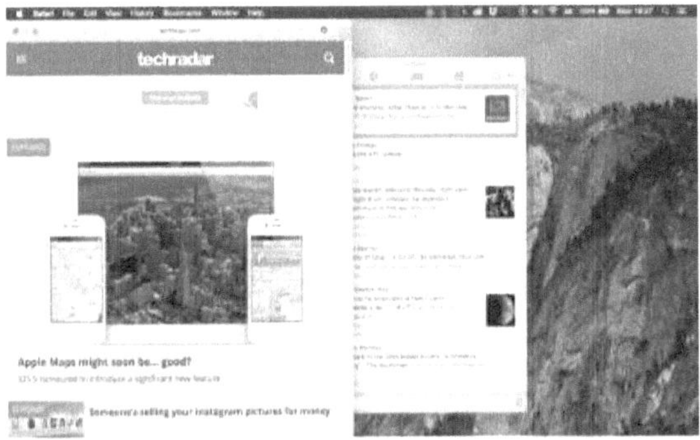

Be adaptable with regards to your windows in macOS/OS X. You can drag from whichever side to resize, but that's not all as you can likewise press Option to resize from different sides at the same time (from the dragged window and the side facing it). You can also press Shift to resize while locking it.

• **Conceal a Window** - To rapidly conceal a window on the work area, simply press Command + H. The application will vanish. However, you could recall it by tapping on the symbol on the Dock or utilizing Command + Tab.

- **Conceal All Windows** - You can conceal the entirety of windows except the "window for the app" that's currently in use, by holding "Option + Command + H."

48. Check your activities on Mac using Activity Monitor

If you discover that your Mac is getting slow, or maybe the fans are on, and you aren't doing something too intensive, you can check to know the cause of the problem. "Activity Monitor" in OS X/macOS reveals your Mac details and how they are being utilized.

On the "Activity Monitor" inside the "Utilities folder" to check the programs on your device and the resources they consume.

The sections display vital data like your CPU usage of a procedure or the RAM it consumes. If there's a procedure that is hoarding resources, and you don't need it, you can kill it off by picking it and pressing the "Quit Process."

In case you're only curious as to the usage of your systems' resources, tap on the tabs (System memory, CPU, etc.) to see diagram displaying the usage over time.

49. Separate the "external hard drives" in Disk Utility

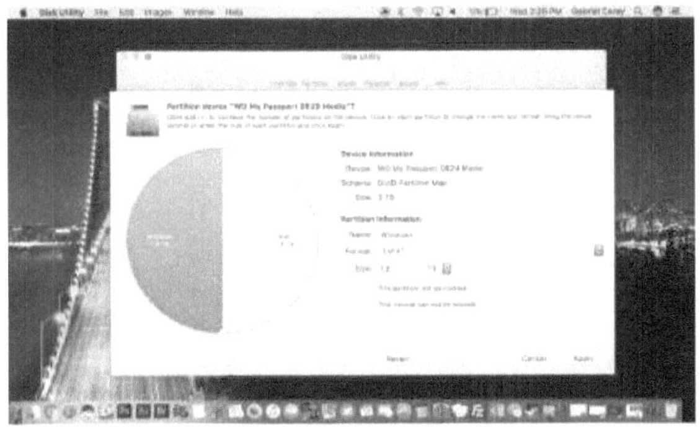

One hidden fact about Mac is, by default, it utilizes an alternate file system than the Windows PCs.

That implies that in case you're going to share an "external hard drive" between Apple's and Microsoft's OS, you have a couple of alternatives. You can format your hard drive to exploit the "exFAT file system" and consequently pass up on quicker write times.

Fortunately, in the Disk Utility application in macOS, you have the option to divide hard drives. In doing as such, you can hypothetically partition the drive into two and have one volume committed to macOS and the second for

Windows.

50. Back up the Mac device

We realize that individuals haven't forgotten how to back up their Mac; however, we also realize that such a significant number of individuals try not to. You should do this. Since the time of "OS X 10.5," Apple has simplified backing-up through the use of Time Machine. You ought to do different things to back up your Mac; however, you should use the Time Machine; users can get a 2TB drive for under sixty quid. Ensure to do this now.

51.   Initiate Spotlight to Search - To display a convenient search interface to enable you to discover records in your Mac system, simply use Command + Space. "Spotlight" can do a wide range of things, from finding documents to responding to fundamental inquiries and also solving math questions.

52.   Interchange Between Apps - To swap between the open apps, press Command + Tab. Hold down on the Command key and afterward tap Tab to go through the open applications. Release the button when the application you need is highlighted.

53. Cycle among App Windows – When you have different windows running for an application like Safari, interchanging among those windows is possible simply press "Command + the Tilde (~)" key.

54. Change Between various Desktops - If you utilize different desktops, you can interchange between them rapidly by pressing the Control tab and afterward press either the right or the left arrow.

Managing Files

55. Instantly Open Folders - To open up folders in the Finder or from the desktop, press Command, and then hold the arrow key. To return, simply hold Command then tap on up arrow key.

56. Clear your Desktop – For users using "macOS Mjave" or later, on an untidy desktop, simply right tap and pick "Stacks" to have Mac instantly arrange everything.

57. Quick File Deletion - If you need to erase a document and need to sidestep the Trash Can on your Mac that saves records before erasing them, simply select a document and tap "Option + Command +Delete" simultaneously.

58. Turn off Applications from App Switcher – While in the "Command + Tab view," tap on "Q" key and hold down on Command to close-off open applications.

59. Hot corners – In case you're not already utilizing Hot corners, they're cool. From there, users can set tasks to function whenever the mouse floats in a particular corner, for example, launching "Mission Control," displaying your desktop, and so on. To configure Hot Corners, go to System Preferences, Mission Control then Hot Corners.

60. Advanced Hot Corners – In case you need to utilize Hot Corners, but you've unknowingly been activating features, simply press down the "Option" key while you configure it. Note that Hot Corner will not activate if you're not pressing down the Option key.

61. Conceal a window – To conceal a window, simply tap Command + H. the application will vanish within the background. However, you can always regain it by tapping the symbol on the Dock or pressing Command + Tab.

62. Conceal all Windows - To rapidly conceal all windows apart from the window for the application you're utilizing, simply press Option + Command + H.

63. Make an Auto Duplicating document

- If you need to make a copy record while tapping on a particular document, right-click then pick "Get Info." And afterward check the "Stationary Pad box." Each time you open that document, it will create and open a copy, which is incredible for layouts and comparable file types.

64. Quick Looks - When utilizing your Mac with "Force Touch Trackpad," If you tap & hold on something, let's say a link to a site or a video, you'll get a little preview of the file without leaving the present page you're on.

65. Password Authentication with Apple Watch - For users on "macOS Catalina" and Apple Watch, the Watch can likewise be utilized as an option to a secret word so you wouldn't have to type in passwords much of the time.

Notification Center

66. Activating the DND Quickly - If you press down on the Options button and tap on the "Notification Center" symbol by the upper right corner of the menu bar on your Mac, you can actuate "Do Not Disturb."

Keyboard Tricks

67. Alternating Mouse Control - There's an alternative to controlling the mouse cursor using your keyboard, and you can turn it on in Accessibility. Open "Accessibility settings" and under "Pointer Control," opick "Alternate Control Methods."

Afterward, activate "Enable Mouse Keys" and choose "toggle to turn on Mouse Keys when Option is pressed 5otimes". Whenever you press Option five times, Mouse Keys switch on; then, you can utilize the console to move your mouse.

68. Fast Access to "Function Key Settings"

While you click a function key to enact "Mission Control," Media playback, Brightness and so on, if you press down the Option key, you can get to the Settings options in "System Preferences" for those particular keys. Remember that this does not go well with" Touch Bar Macs."

69. **Dictionary** - If you view a new word that you're curious about, Highlight the word then press down on it using the "Force Touch

Trackpad" to get its definition.

70. Rename Folders & documents-

If you "Force Touch Trackpad" on any file or folder name, you can rapidly rename it. "Force Touch" on any folder or document symbol, and you'll get a preview of it.

Apple Watch & Mac

71.   To unlock using Apple Watch

In case you possess an Apple Watch, you can utilize it to open your Mac, which is a very helpful component for the individuals who don't know. To configure this, open "System Preferences"> "Security and Privacy" then switch on

"Unlock Mac with Apple Watch."

Safari

72. Safari (Picture within a Picture) for

YouTube - You can view one video in Safari just as you are doing something else. This can be done with YouTube by tapping on a video twice while it's playing to display a menu showing the "picture in-picture" function.

73. The Apple Mac "Finder" option

Use the "Finder" on your Apple Mac to arrange your documents so you can locate them easily. If you want to open a "Finder" window, apply the Finder symbol in the Dock which you will see below the home screen. Force click (add pressure to the click) a folder icon to display the items instantly, or do that for a filename you want to edit.

74. Safari "Picture-in-Picture" Part two

In case the right-clicking technique does not perform the function of bring-out a video, there's a second strategy. While a video plays, locate the audio symbol in the "Safari toolbar" then right-tap to enable it to bring out the "picture in-picture" option.

75. Easy way to copy a Link – Whenever you need to copy the present URL while using Safari, tap "Command + L" to highlight the URL then tap "Command + C" to copy. It's faster than utilizing a mouse.

76. Use Dark Mode for Focus

Use a dark color theme for the screen, menu panel, dock, as well as all macOS apps that are pre-installed. Your content appears boldly from the middle and front as the darkened indicators and windows stay in the background. In apps like Gmail, Contact details, Calendar, and SMS, you can display text content with white on a dark background. This makes it better for your eyes when typing at night.

"Dark Mode" is perfectly designed for specialists editing pictures and images— hues and technical aspects display against the textures of the dark app; however, the feature is also perfect for someone who just needs to concentrate on their work.

77. Sync other Apple devices

You will find a device in the "Finder" sidebar if you link such a device (iPhone or iPad). At that location, your device can be backed up, updated and restored.

Display with "Gallery." A wide display of a chosen folder can be seen with "Gallery View," which offers you a simple way to clearly recognize photos, film clips, as well as other files.

The "Preview" pane displays advice to assist you to identify the folder you are looking for. To easily find what you're searching for, use the scrubber bar that you will find below the screen — type "Shift-Command-P" to close or open the "Preview" table.

Suggestion: Tap "Command-J" andopick "Show filename" to display file names under the "Gallery View."

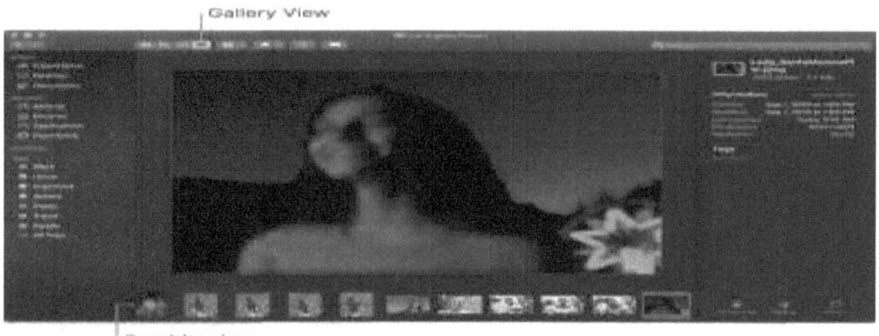

78. Quick Actions

There are shortcuts at the lower right corner of the "Preview" pane that allow you to access and update documents inside the "Finder." In Markup, you can transform a picture, analyze or edit a portrait, merge photos including PDFs into one file, clip mp3, and mp4 documents, and create unique behavior via Automator workflows (e.g., watermarking a folder). To see the alternatives of the "Preview" panel in the

"Finder," click "View" > Display "Preview." Select "View" > Display "Preview Options" if you want to configure what can be seen.

Afterward, pick your file type preferences.

Suggestion: To launch "Quick Look," pick a folder and touch the "Space bar." Without launching a different application, you can register PDFs, clip mp3 and mp4 files; and tag, tilt and clip photos.

79. View All of an Application's Open Windows

To use "Exposé," Pressure click an icon in the Dock to display every open window of the app.

Advice: You can create a bigger or smaller dock, include or delete objects, switch it to the display's back or side, and even program it to disappear when it is inactive. Tap the "System Preferences" symbol in the Dock t oadjust your Dock settings or pick the Apple menu >"System Preferences."

Tap on the "Dock."

80. Launch Apps on Your Mac Easily

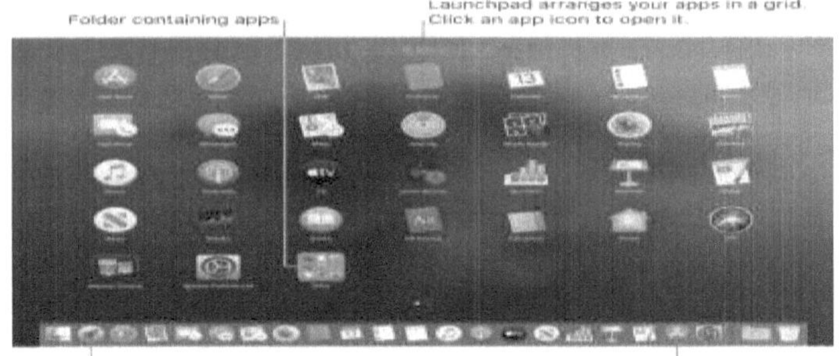

Your IMac functions with apps for everything you enjoy doing — web browsing, checking emails, sharing pictures, enjoying films and shows, etc.

81. Launch an application

Tap the Dock's app icon or tap the Dock's Launchpad icon and press the desired program.

You may use "Spotlight" too look for an application, then launch the appoimmediately from the search findings of "Spotlight."

Ask Siri. Say: "Open Calculator."

82. The Dock on Your Computer

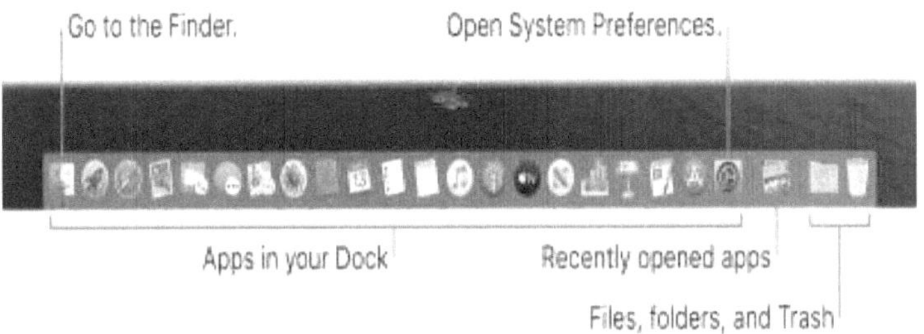

The Dock below the screen is a sensible location for storing apps and files that you often use

83. Access a file or App

Tap the app's icon, which is found in the Dock. Apps you just launched appear in the Dock's central page.

84. Include an object in the Dock

Drag and drop the object where you'd like it — position apps in the left part of the Dock. For documents and folders, place them in the right corner.

85. Take an object out of the Dock

Pull it from the Dock Although; the object is extracted from the Dock, It is still on your computer.

86. Notification Center on your Apple Mac

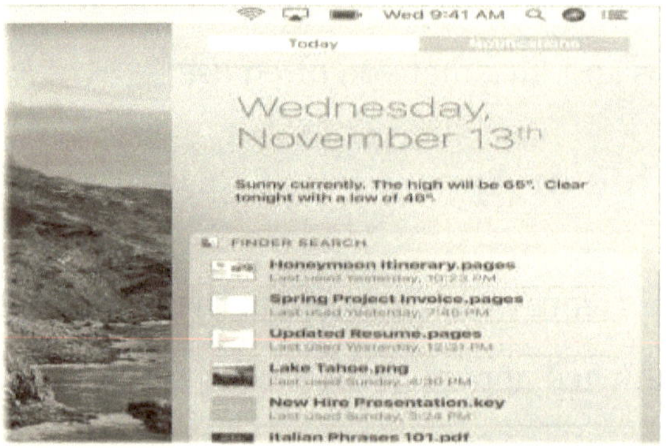

Using Notification Center to display information in your day (schedule, inventory, climate, etc.) and pick up the pace on alerts that you may have forgotten (mails, alerts, device updates, etc.).

87. Launch Notification Center

At the upper right corner of the screen, press the "Notification Center" button. Tap "Today" to see what will happen, or Notifications to check what will happen.

88. Silence Notifications

Launch Notification Center, move up, and switch on "Do Not Disturb." After launching, you won't be able to view or recognize updates, but it will be in the Notification Center to be viewed later.

89. System Preferences

You can change your MacBook Pro configuration using System Preferences on your computer. For instance, to switch sleep arrangements, use "Energy Saver" settings. Or use "Desktop & Screen Saver" settings to add a desktop image or select a background image.

90. Customize your AppleiMac

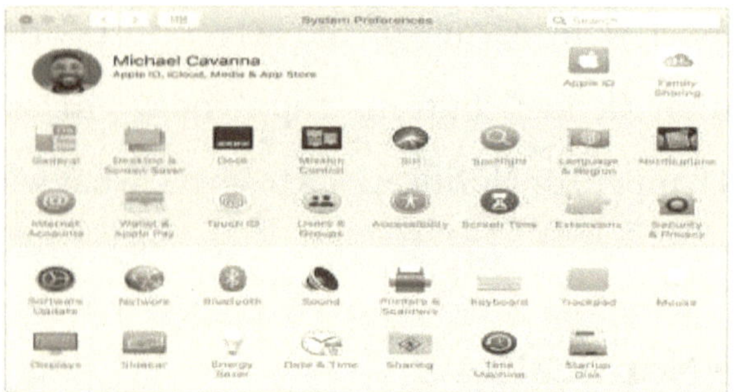

Tap on the Dock's "System Preferences" button or pick the Apple menu and go to "System

Preferences." Then click on the preferences you would like to develop.

Upgrade macOSPressothe Dock's "System Preferences" symbol, then select "Software Update" to check if the current version of macOS apps is operating on your Apple computer.

91. Apple Mac Spotlight

The Spotlight logo is a good way of finding something like files, addresses, calendar events, and text messages on your computer. Spotlight Tips gives information from wikipedia pages, internet search information, news, events, climate, investment news, films, and other outlets. When searching via Spotlight, the preview gives indexed lists you can communicate with. For instance, call someone, email a friend, play a tune, find the direction to a destination, even find monetary conversion rates.

Spotlight can give answers to math calculations or characterize words, all in your work area.

92. Switch on Siri

Press the —Siri‖ symbol in the menu bar; at that point tap —Enable when prompted.‖ In the event that you empowered Siri during configuration, tapping the symbol opens Siri. Or on the other hand, press the —System

Preferences‖ symbol in the Dock > tap —Siri, ‖ at that point, choose —Enable Ask Siri."

You can change different settings in the Siri sheet, for example, the Language and whether to place the Siri logo in the menu bar.

Note: To utilize Siri, your computer must be enabled with internet connections.

93. Address Siri

Click on the —Siri‖ symbol from the menu bar and begin your request. Or then again force click the

—Command-Space bar, ‖ and say something to Siri.

94. Hey Siri

Saying "Hey Siri" onto your Apple MacBook will get you answers to the spoken request. To turn this option on, head over to —System

Preferences" and open the Siri panel.

Press "Listen for 'Hey Siri,'" at that point, and say a few Siri directions after every prompt. For comfort, this command will not work when the cover of your device is not opened.

Tip: Find out about the different ways you can utilize Siri, ask, "What would you do?" whenever, or use the Help key.

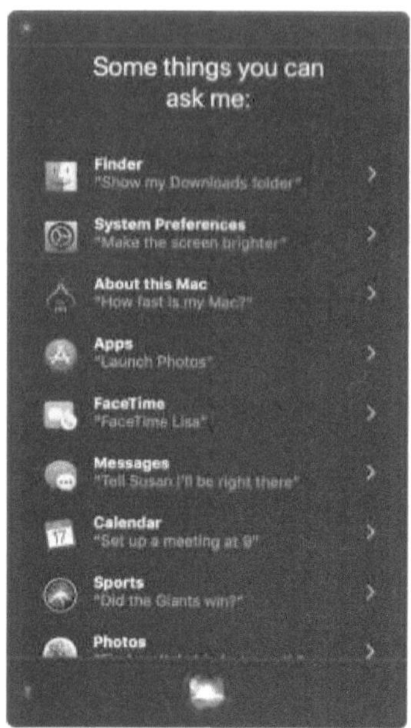

95. Listen to songs with Siri

Simply tell it to, "Play some music," and Siri opens the music app. Also, tell it to, "Play the top songs from June 2000."

96. Look for files with Siri

Tell Siri to discover documents and open it directly from its panel. You can use filename or description to make this request. For instance, "Give me

88

documents David requested," or "Open the file I made the previous evening."

97. Find Anything from Your Search

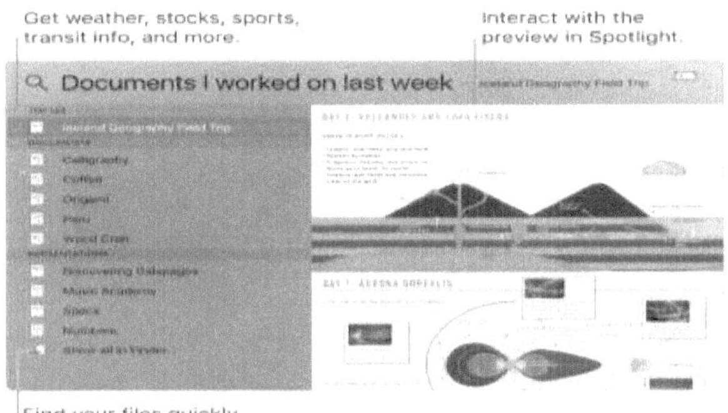

Press the —Spotlight‖ symbol at the upper right of the screen; start composing afterward.

Tip: Enter —Command–Space bar‖ to reveal or expose the Spotlight search area.

98. Get flight information

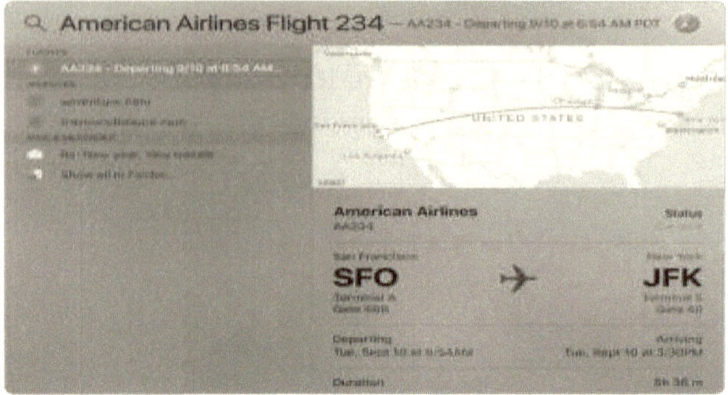

You don't need to launch Safari to see flight status. With Spotlight, all you need to do is type the aircraft and flight number, and you will see your flight status and map.

See your search results. Click on a search box to check it out on the preview on the right side. In some cases, that isoall you have to do—click bookmarks or web links from the preview. You can likewise double tap a search result to see the content.

99. Siri on your Mac

Converse with Siri on your Apple IMac and utilize your unique sound for some apps. For instance, you can discover folders, plan gatherings, configuration settings, get solutions, send SMS, make phone calls, and include objects to your schedule. Siri will offer you directions ("How would I return home from my office?"), give data ("How tallois Mt. Everest?"), perform essential errands ("Start another basic food item list"), and considerably more.

From your Apple Mac, Siri is accessible at whatever point you state, "Hey Siri," and quickly make your request (make sure you open the cover of your Apple MacBook). Play a song, organize a get-together, search for a folder, and more by speaking your request. You can empower the "Listen for 'Hey Siri'" feature in the —Siri‖ window of System Preferences.

Note: Siri may not be accessible in all dialects or in all territories, and highlights may change by territory.

100. Intuitive with Siri

Drag and drop pictures and areas from the Siri panel into an email, instant message, or report.

You can copy and paste documents.

101. Pin an outcome

Save the Search outcome of Siri from games, Reminders, Watch, Investments, Notes, Finder, and general information (Google, for instance) to the Today see in —Notifications.‖ Press the addition ‗+' sign in the upper right of a Siri result to stick it to the —Today View." Check it later by clicking the —Notification Center" symbol, then tap —Today.‖ In case you're looking for a game's score, for instance, results will be refreshed.

102. Use another voice

Tap the —System Preferences‖ symbol in the Dock > tap —Siri.‖ Afterward, from the —Siri Voice‖ menu, pick your desired option.

All through this guide, you'll discover recommendations for things you can request from Siri, and they include:

Ask Siri. Make a request such as:

"Open the Key note introduction I was taking a shot at the previous evening." —What time is it in London?"